ISBN 978-1-332-27862-6
PIBN 10308160

1 MONTH OF FREE READING

at
www.ForgottenBooks.com

By purchasing this book you are eligible for one month membership to ForgottenBooks.com, giving you unlimited access to our entire collection of over 700,000 titles via our web site and mobile apps.

To claim your free month visit:

www.forgottenbooks.com/free308160

Similar Books Are Available from
www.forgottenbooks.com

THE RELEVANCE OF KAHNEMAN AND TVERSKY'S

CONCEPT OF FRAMING TO ORGANIZATION BEHAVIOR[1]

Max H. Bazerman

December, 1983   WP# 1510-83

Journal of Management, in Press

THE RELEVANCE OF KAHNEMAN AND TVERSKY'S
CONCEPT OF FRAMING TO ORGANIZATION BEHAVIOR[1]

Max H. Bazerman

Massachusetts Institute of Technology

1. This research was funded by National Science Foundation Grant BNS-8107331. The author benefitted from numerous insightful comments from Ed Conlon, Terry Connelly, Kathy Kram, John Martin, Phil Mirvis, and two anonymous reviewers. Correspondence should be sent to Max H. Bazerman, Massachusetts Institute of Technology, Sloan School of Management, 50 Memorial Drive, Cambridge, MA, 02139.

The Relevance of Kahneman and Tversky's Concept of
Framing to Organizational Behavior

Abstract

Recent research by Kahneman and Tversky (1979) has demonstrated that
individual decisions are <u>systematically</u> affected by the way in which problems
are presented. Specifically, individuals tend to be risk averse to problems
framed in the positive direction (i.e., concerning gains) and to be risk
seeking to problems framed in the negative direction (i.e., concerning
losses). This paper (1) demonstrates that this concept of framing has wide
explanatory power concerning a variety of concepts in organizational behavior
and (2) argues that the framing of experimental materials affects the
formation of paradigms in organizational behavior. It is argued that many
accepted "findings" may exist more because of the way researchers frame the
problem than because of the presumed impact of the construct on individual
behavior. Specific application is provided to the areas of (1) the escalation
of commitment, (2) negotiator behavior and (3) "the risky shift."

The Relevance of Kahneman and Tversky's Concept of Framing to Organizational Behavior

Traditional models and theories in organizational behavior have dealt with how individuals respond to various situations. Rarely have we concerned ourselves, however, with the way situations are framed to the target individual or group. Consider the following problem context (modified from Kahneman and Tversky [1982]):

> A large car manufacturer has recently been hit with a number of economic difficulties and it appears as if three plants need to be closed and 6000 employees laid off. The vice-president of production has been exploring alternative ways to avoid this crisis. She has developed two plans:
>
> Plan A: This plan will save 1 of the 3 plants and 2000 jobs.
>
> Plan B: This plan has a 1/3 probability of saving all 3 plants and all 6000 jobs, but has a 2/3 probability of saving no plants and no jobs.
>
> Which plan would you select?

Organizational behavior has given us a number of issues to consider. What will be the impact of each action on the union? What will be the impact of each plan on the motivation and morale of retained employees? How do the values of the vice-president of production differ from those of the larger corporation? While all of these questions are important and have been addressed in the organizational behavior literature, a more fundamental question underlies the subjective situation and the resulting decision. Reconsider the above problem, replacing the choices provided above with the following choices:

> Plan C: This plan will result in the loss of 2 of the 3 plants and 4000 jobs.
>
> Plan D: This plan has a 2/3 probability of resulting in the loss of all 3 plants and all 6000 jobs, but has a 1/3 probability of losing no plants and no jobs.
>
> Which plan would you select?

Close examination of the two sets of alternative plans finds them to be objectively the same. However, most (80+%) individuals choose Plan A (objectively the same as Plan C) in the first set, while most (80+%) individuals choose Plan D (objectively the same as Plan B) in the second set (Bazerman, 1985). Changing the description of the outcome states from job and plants saved (gains) to jobs and plants lost (losses) was sufficient to shift prototypic choice from risk averse (take the sure thing) to risk seeking. Why do (aggregated) individuals demonstrate this apparent contradiction? The theory that explains this pattern of choice underlies our examination of the impact of "framing" on the field of organizational behavior.

This shift in prototypical choice is inconsistent with expected utility theory (von Neumann & Morganstern, 1947; Holloway, 1979), but is consistent with a growing body of literature (Kahneman & Tversky, 1979, 1982; Tversky & Kahneman, 1981; Thaler, 1980) which shows that individuals treat risks concerning perceived gains (e.g., saving jobs and plants -- see plans A & B) differently from risks concerning perceived losses (e.g., losing jobs and plants -- see plans C & D). In an attempt to explain these common and systematic deviations from rationality, Kahneman and Tversky (1979) developed "Prospect Theory". This theory suggests (1) rewards and losses are evaluated relative to a neutral reference point, (2) potential outcomes are expressed as gains (e.g., jobs and plants saved) or losses (e.g., jobs and plants lost) relative to this fixed, neutral reference point and (3) the resultant change in the asset position is assessed by an S-shaped value function (see Figure 1). While there are a number of additional tenets of prospect theory (e.g., the response to losses is more extreme than the response to gains), we will limit our attention to the issues identified above.

As demonstrated in Figure 1, decisions made tend to avoid risk with regards to gains and seek risk with regards to losses. For example, this curve suggests that most individuals would choose a $10,000,000 gain for sure over a 50% chance of getting a $20,000,000 gain, since the value placed on $20,000,000 is not twice as great as the value placed on $10,000,000. In addition, this curve suggests that most individuals would choose a 50% chance of a $20,000,000 loss over a sure loss of $10,000,000 since the negative value placed on $20,000,000 is not twice as great as the negative value placed on $10,000,000. This part of Tversky and Kahneman's logic is consistent with classical utility theory. They add, however, that the way the problem is framed, or presented, can dramatically change the perceived neutral point of the question. Thus, in the above example, if the problem is framed in terms of losing jobs and plants, the current position is neutral, the choices are evaluated on the loss part of the curve and risk seeking behavior results. That is, if we think in terms of losing jobs, the negative value placed on the loss of 3 plants and 6000 jobs is viewed (by most individuals) as not being three times as negative as losing 1 plant and 2000 jobs (see Figure 1). However, if the problem is framed in terms of saving jobs and plants, the potential disaster (losing everything) becomes the neutral point, the choices are evaluated on the gain part of the curve and risk averse behavior results. Within this alternative frame, Figure 1 clarifies that the gain placed on saving 3 plants and 6000 jobs is viewed (by most individuals) as not being three times as great as saving 1 plant and 2000 jobs. The key point is that Kahneman and Tversky (1979) identified a systematic pattern of how the framing of the problem will affect the subsequent decision.

This paper delineates the power of Kahneman and Tversky's theory of decision behavior for explaining constructs within the domain of

organizational behavior. Specifically, it will be suggested that many well accepted "findings" may exist more because of the way researchers framed the problem than because of the presumed impact of the construct on the behavior of subjects. The remainder of this paper will attempt to show how this one form of problem framing identified by Kahneman and Tversky (1979) explains decisions across three conceptual domains.

The following three sections of the paper examine the relevance of framing to (1) the growing literature on the escalation of commitment to a previous course of action; (2) concessionary behavior by negotiators; and (3) the risky shift paradigm. In each part, the literature will be selectively reviewed, the insights provided by the concept of framing will be identified, and the importance of these insights for future research will be considered. Finally, a concluding section integrates the discussion of the role of framing in organizational behavior. A key theme that is developed concerns the need to create paradigms that separate the impact of (1) the researchers suggested objective independent variable state and (2) the way the problem is framed to the subject.

Escalation of Commitment

You have personally decided to hire a new middle level manager in your firm. While you expected excellent performance, the early information suggests that she is not performing as expected. Should you fire her? Perhaps you really can't afford her current level of performance. On the other hand, you have invested a fair amount in her development. Furthermore, she may just be in the process of learning the ropes. So you decide to invest in her a bit longer and provide additional resources so that she can succeed. Again she does not perform as expected. Although you have more reason to "cut your losses," you now have even more invested in this employee. This pattern

goes on for the next two years. When do you give up on your "investment"?
All of us have spent too much time in this kind of trap.

Staw and his associates (cf., Staw, 1976, 1981); among others (Teger,
1980; Brockner and Rubin, 1984; Bazerman, Beekun and Schoorman, 1982; Conlon
and Wolf, 1980), have demonstrated that decision-makers who commit themselves
to a particular course of action may commit added resources in a non-optimal
way in order to justify the previous commitment. This justification process
has serious implications for financial, managerial and political decisions.
This section of the paper seeks to theoretically demonstrate the importance of
problem framing on the tendency to escalate previous commitment.

The experimental demonstration of the tendency to escalate commitment has
typically involved the simulation of a decision process (e.g., Staw, 1976).
An experimental group is asked to make a choice between two investment
options. The simulation continues by informing the participants that several
years later their investment has not been successful but that they have the
option of investing more money in the venture. A control group is told of a
decision made by another individual which has not been successful and is also
given the option of investing more money in the venture. Staw (1976) reported
that with groups of business school students playing the role of a financial
vice president making investment decisions in R & D programs, the experimental
group consistently allocated more money to the previously chosen venture than
did the control group. A critical conclusion made by most escalation
researchers (e.g., Bazerman, Giuliano and Appelman, in press) is that the
tendency to escalate represents a deviation from optimal decision making.

In contrast to the conclusion that decision-makers are acting
irrationally, the framework outlined in Figure 1 provides an alternative

explanation of escalatory behavior (e.g., Staw's results). Consider the
subject in Staw's research that made an initial allocation decision to one of
the two investment options, and that after three years was at a loss position
on that investment of negative $10 million. On the graph this represents a
perceived loss of 165 value units. Interestingly, an added loss of $10
million would only have a further negative affect on your value assessment of
35 units. Consequently, the subject would be likely to risk an additional $10
million for a 50% chance of recapturing the initial investment. In contrast,
a new decision-maker is likely to reassess the situation from a new neutral
reference point. That is, he/she will not necessarily view the decision from
the loss portion of the utility curve. Consequently, he/she will be less
affected by the initial decision. Accepting utility theory as representing
reasonable behavior (i.e., it maximizes expected utility), this analysis
questions the existence of nonrationality in the results of previous
escalation research. That is, it would appear that subjects in previous
escalation experimentation may simply have been acting according to the
rational model specified by the classical utility model.

The nonrationality of subjects in an escalation situation, however, comes
into play when we consider the theoretically predicted impact of the way the
escalation problem has been framed in the existing literature. The subject in
the escalation paradigm has been told that the initial investment has not
produced the desired results (i.e., it has been lost), leading subjects to
evaluate the feedback on the left-hand side of the curve in Figure 1.
Alternatively, subjects could be led to view the second decision separately
from the first decision, putting the decision-maker back to the neutral
reference point. Finally, in sharp contrast to the existing frame, if the
research funding comes out of a special source of funds, the feedback could be

presented in terms of "you still have X million of research funds available"
(gain part of curve, positive frame), rather than "you have lost Y million"
(loss part of curve, negative frame). This alternative framing is likely to
result in a shift from risk seeking behavior (adding more to the investment)
to risk averse behavior (accepting the sure loss).

The above analysis discusses framing from the perspective of how the
information is presented to the decision-maker. The behavioral sciences
recognize, however, that individuals reinterpret information. Following this
pattern, decision-makers are likely to have varying tendencies in terms of the
frame they typically adopt. Thus, the combination of information format
presented and the individual's framing tendencies will affect risk attitudes
and subsequent escalation behavior of managers, politicians and academicians.

In summary, the escalation paradigm is an important new direction in
decision making research. The current theory suggests an alternative view of
the existing data on escalation, and suggests that we need to separate the
impact of (1) the objective state in the escalation paradigm from (2) the
frame used to influence the subject. Recalling Staw's (1976) classic
experiment ("Knee-Deep in the Big Muddy..."), we question whether the
escalation effect would be observed if the study examined the problem from the
frame of "having 75% of your body out of the mud."

Negotiation

Over the past 20 years, negotiation research has been dominated by two
sets of forces, collective bargaining research in labor relations and social
psychology. Unfortunately, this literature has failed to consider the process
of decision making under competitive conditions. This section seeks to show
that such a perspective is a critical new direction for negotiation reseach,

and that the specific effects of the negotiator's frame has impressive potential for clarifying paradoxes within the negotiation setting.

Farber and Katz (1979) have recently identified the importance of risk attitudes of negotiators under conditions of binding arbitration. In binding arbitration, both sides agree, or are legally compelled, to have a third party impose a resolution if the two sides fail to reach a resolution on their own. Arbitration has the benefits of replacing the harmful effects of a strike, while encouraging the parties to agree in order to avoid the uncertainty associated with the binding decision of a third party. Arbitration has become an increasingly common form of dispute resolution, both in the public and private sectors (Kochan, 1980).

Farber and Katz (1979) suggest that if both parties are risk averse, then negotiators should reach a negotiated settlement (i.e., take the sure thing), rather than impose arbitration (a riskier option — without increasing the aggregated expected value). A resolution is also predicted if one party is sufficiently risk averse such that they are willing to pay the premium required by the more risk seeking party to forego the uncertainty inherent in arbitration. Conversely, if both parties are risk seeking, then arbitration will be invoked. To summarize, in order for arbitration to be normatively invoked, a risk seeking preference must aggregately exist between the two parties. In addition, it is widely accepted in the decision theory literature that individuals and organizations tend to be risk averse (Holloway, 1979). The paradox is obvious -- if arbitration is a risk seeking alternative, why do typically risk averse individuals and/or organizations exhibit increasing utilization of arbitrators? It is argued below that the frame of negotiators is critical in clarifying this paradoxical state.

Consider a prototypic labor-management situation: The union claims they need a raise to $12/hour, and that anything less would represent a loss to members given the current inflationary environment. Management, in contrast, claims that they cannot pay more than $10/hour, and that anything more would impose an unacceptable loss to the company. In our simplified one issue case, what if each side had the option of settling for $11/hour or going to arbitration? Since each party is viewing the negotiation in terms of what they have to lose, following Kahneman and Tversky's (1979) basic propositions, each will respond in a risk seeking manner and arbitration is likely to be chosen. Given the same objective specified above, but changing the subjective gain/loss situation results in a very different predicted outcome. If the union views anything above $10/hour as a gain and management views anything under $12/hour as a gain, then a positive frame will exist, risk aversion will tend to dominate and a negotiated settlement will generally occur.

The implication of the above framework is of critical importance. Both sides in negotiations often talk in terms of why they need a certain wage -- they talk in terms of losses. What if they believe themselves? The above scenario provides the answer! They will adopt a negative frame and exhibit risk seeking behavior (Bazerman and Neale, 1983; Bazerman, in press). Neale and Bazerman (1983) found that labor/management negotiators with positive frames are significantly more concessionary and successful than their negatively framed counterparts. Similarly, Bazerman, Magliozzi, and Neale (1983) found that buyers and sellers who adopt a positive frame are able to complete transactions more quickly and are significantly more successful than those who adopt a negative frame. A critical role of mediators and other interested third parties should be to encourage both parties to view the conflict in a positive (or at least neutral) frame. Finally, while the above framework was developed in the

labor-management domain, the framing perspective of conflict is relevant to any negotiation context in which two parties have the option of accepting a settlement or in some way risking the escalation of the dispute (e.g., divorce, transfer pricing, salary negotiation, etc.).

The Framing of a Paradigm — The Case of the Risky Shift

Earlier sections of this paper have examined how the framing of problems would affect judgment in the escalation paradigm and within competitive situations. This section examines the much reviewed "risky shift" paradigm (cf. Cartwright, 1973) in an attempt to show how an entire research paradigm involving nearly 200 researchers may have been framed. Attention is shifted towards showing how framing affects the decisions of researchers, rather than a generic class of decisions as in the previous sections. This paper suggests that the frame used by Stoner's (1961) initial study may have been a critical biasing influence on the risky shift paradigm and the area of group decision processes.

Over the past twenty years, considerable evidence has been added to Stoner's (1961) initial demonstration that groups make riskier decisions than the mean of the decisions previously made by the individual members of that group. Rarely in the history of the behavioral sciences has a single laboratory study stimulated as much empirical research as Stoner's (1961) study of the risky shift. As findings began to accumulate, it became clear that the shift observed by Stoner (1961) using the Choice Dilemma Questionnaire (CDQ) as a means of operationalizing risk produced replicable results. The CDQ consists of 12 hypothetical choice dilemmas, each of which requires the focal subject (either individual or group) to select the minimum probability of success such that they would recommend a particular risky

choice. Historically, the twelve probabilities were summed, to give a single score in which a lower score designated a riskier course of action.

Although the risky shift, using the CDQ, has been remarkably stable across a wide variety of experimental settings and types of experimental subjects, the shift for the various items of the CDQ differ substantially both in direction and magnitude. Some items consistently produce risky shifts, some items produce no significant shift, and two items regularly generate cautious shifts (i.e., the groups are less risky than individuals). In addition, new items similar in form to the CDQ have been constructed and tested which consistently generate cautious shifts (Cartwright, 1973).

Added questions concerning the risky shift paradigm were provided by contradictory research in "real-life" situations (e.g., investors, juries, consumers) and laboratory research that did not employ the CDQ. Sometimes a risky shift occurred, sometimes a cautious shift occurred and sometimes no shift occurred. Based on such evidence, Cartwright (1973) concluded that "it is now evident that the persistent search for an explanation of 'the risky shift' was misdirected and that any adequate theory will have to account for a much more complicated set of data than originally anticipated" (pg. 45).

The above stated fixation on laboratory studies using the CDQ has obscured the most critical question: When does a risky versus cautious shift occur? The black-box approach of using the total CDQ score is incapable of delineating the processes underlying group induced risk shifts. In a unique attempt to explain when risky versus cautious shifts will predictably be induced, Vinokur (1971) suggested that individuals and groups will choose that option which maximizes their expected utility. While interesting, this idea fails to clarify the conditions under which the maximization of subjective expected utility will lead to risky versus cautious shifts. Clarification of

this question comes from the framing concept. As suggested earlier, in comparison to maximizing expected value (the straight line in Figure 1), individuals will tend to be risk averse in positively framed situations, while being risk seeking in negatively framed situations. We might hypothesize, however, that groups encourage the verbalization of the problem in multiple alternative frames by varying group members -- thus diluting the impact of any one specific frame. This suggests that groups will move away from the classical utility curve towards an expected value (or risk neutral) decision strategy. Examining Figure 1, this perspective would suggest that (1) judgments made by individuals will tend to follow the classical utility curve and (2) group decisions will tend to adjust towards the risk neutral line. This analysis would predict a risky shift on positively framed items and a cautious shift on negatively framed items. Subject to empirical validation, this analysis has the potential for clarifying group induced shifts and the existence of the risky shift paradigm. Examination of the CDQ finds that this instrument is positively framed, which leads to the prediction of a risky shift. Would we currently be re-examining "the cautious shift" paradigm had Stoner (1961) initially conducted his experiment with a negatively framed instrument?

The current perspective suggests that the entire paradigm may have been established by the generally positive frame of the CDQ and Stoner's (1961) initial use of this instrument. Following Stoner's (1961) research, his initial conclusion continues to permeate introductory textbooks and the folklore of group decision making. If an entire body of research can be framed, we can only be awed by the extent to which individual researchers will be biased by the way we ask our research questions.

The Future Role of Framing in Organizational Behavior

In the sections above, three research topics to which the framing concept is relevant were identified. It is suggested that the framing concept can (1) clarify additional paradoxes in our field and (2) increase our understanding of existing theories. Expectancy theory (cf. Mitchell, 1974), for example, makes a number of assumptions that Prospect Theory addresses. In most common formulations of expectancy theory, value is the central concept, rather than utility. The arguments in favor of utility are persuasive (von Neumann & Morganstern, 1947; Holloway, 1979). In addition, expectancy theory assumes that the reference point for evaluating alternative courses of action is not critical. Kahneman and Tversky's (1979) Prospect Theory, in contrast, would suggest that this reference point is crucial, particularly in evaluating the motivational forces associated with alternative actions with varying degrees of risk. That is, Prospect Theory would suggest that the order preferences between two choices of behavior may depend on the framing of the motivational forces of the alternative choices. Many of the most powerful theories in organizational behavior have been developed with a number of assumptions. Our most critical _future_ developments may be created by unraveling such assumptions.

In addition to its relevancy to theoretical frameworks in organizational behavior, the concept of framing has potential for expanding our understanding of applied managerial problems. For illustration purposes, consider the area of job choice:

> An employee with five years of experience since his M.B.A. has a reasonable job, security, and an average salary for someone with his background. He currently has the option of abandoning his current, safe position, and committing himself to a high risk, high opportunity start-up firm. Will he make a job change?

According to the careers literature, common considerations include family situation, current salary, promotion potential, lifestyle, long term aspirations, etc. Prospect theory suggests, however, that a critical factor will be the reference point from which he evaluates the options. A low reference point (where he thinks he should be at this point in his career) will lead to an evaluation on the gain part of the utility curve (see Figure 1) and a risk averse choice (not switching jobs). A high reference point, however, will lead to an evaluation on the loss part of the curve and a risk seeking choice (switching jobs). This analysis is critical in identifying the inappropriate impact that false career expectations can have on employees. Graduate schools and employers, however, frequently create unrealistic career expectations as part of their marketing strategy. This type of analysis is not unique to job choice, rather is intended to highlight the potential of the framing concept to clarify applied managerial situations.

The analyses throughout this paper assume that the problem frame is given. A critical area of inquiry for future research concerns the formation of frames. Most actual problems are not framed in a completely negative or positive frame, as was represented by the problem contexts illustrated in this paper. Rather, individuals often need to interpret the environment and personally frame the problem. Factors such as optimism/pessimism and risk taking propensity are likely to account for individual variation in the framing of problems.

To summarize, by focusing only on the concepts of interest, researchers may make a number of assumptions that have an impact on the conclusions of the research and the subsequent direction of research paradigms. More time should be spent considering the frame and implicit assumptions being made in the initiation stage of research. In his classic paper on the philosophy of

interesting research, Davis (1971) suggests that interesting research is created by questioning the "assumption ground" of the reader. It is suggested here that one definable way of identifying this "assumption ground" is to examine the frame in which a particular paradigm developed. Combining the ideas of Kahneman and Tversky (1979) and Davis (1971), we may find that our most interesting research issues can be discovered by examining the frame of the assumption ground of past research.

References

Bazerman, M. H. Human judgment in managerial decision making, New York: John Wiley and Sons, Inc., 1985.

Bazerman, M.H.   A Critical Look at the Rationality of Negotiator Judgment. American Behavioral Scientist, in press.

Bazerman, M.H., Beekun, R.I., and Schoorman, F.D.   Performance evaluation in a dynamic context: The impact of a prior commitment to the ratee. Journal of Applied Psychology, 1982, 67, 873–876.

Bazerman, M.H., Giuliano, T., and Appelman, A.   Escalation in individual and group decision making. Organizational Behavior and Human Performance, in press.

Bazerman, M. H., & Neale, M. A.   Heuristics in negotiation: Limitations to dispute resolution effectiveness. In M. H. Bazerman & R. J. Lewicki (Eds.), Negotiating in organizations, Beverly Hills: Sage Publishing Inc., 1983.

Bazerman, M.H., Magliozzi, T., and Neale, M.A.   The acquisition of an integrative response in a competitive market. Academy of Management Annual Meeting, 1983.

Bazerman, M. H., & Neale, M. A.   Heuristics in negotiation: Limitations to dispute resolution effectiveness. In M. H. Bazerman & R. J. Lewicki (Eds.), Negotiating in Organizations, Beverly Hills: Sage Publishing Inc., 1983.

Brockner, J., & Rubin, J.Z. The social psychology of entrapment in escalating conflicts, New York: Springer-Verlag, 1984.

Cartwright, D.   Determinants of scientific progress. American Psychologist, 1973, 28, 222–231.

Conlon, E.J., and Wolf, G.   The moderating effects of strategy, visibility and involvement on allocation behavior: An extension of Staw's escalation paradigm. Organizational Behavior and Human Performance. 1980, 26, 172–192.

Davis, M.S.   "That's interesting: Towards a phenomenology of sociology and a sociology of phenomenology," Philosophy of Social Science, 1973, 1, 309–344.

Farber, H., and Katz, H.   Interest arbitration outcomes and the incentives to bargain. Industrial and Labor Relations Review, 1979, 33, 55–63.

Holloway, C.   Decision making under uncertainty: Models and choices, Englewood Cliffs, NJ: Prentice-Hall, 1979.

Kahneman, D., and Tversky, A.   Prospect Theory: An analysis of decision under risk. Econometrica, 1979, 47, 263–291.

Kahneman, D., and Tversky, A. Psychology of preferences. Scientific American, 1982, 161–173.

Kochan, T. Collective bargaining and organizational behavior research. In B. Staw and L. Cummings (eds.) Research in Organizational Behavior, Vol. 2., Greenwich, CT: J.A.I. Press, 1980.

Mitchell, T.R. Expectancy models of job satisfaction, occupational preference and effort: A theoretical, methodological and empirical appraisal. Psychological Bulletin, 1974, 82, 1053–1077.

Neale, M.A., and Bazerman, M.H. Systematic deviations from rationality in negotiator behavior: The framing of conflict and negotiator overconfidence. University of Arizona Working Paper, 1983.

Staw, B.M. Knee-deep in the big muddy: A study of escalating commitment to a chosen course of action. Organizational Behavior and Human Performance, 1976, 16, 27–44.

Staw, B.M.. The escalation of commitment to a course of action. Academy of Management Review, 1981, 6, 577–587.

Stoner, J.A.F. A comparison of individual and group decisions involving risk. Unpublished Master's thesis, Massachusetts Institute of Technology, School of Industrial Management, 1961.

Teger, A. Too much invested to quit, New York: Pergamon Press, 1980.

Thaler, R. Toward a positive theory of consumer choice. Journal of Economic Behavior and Organization, 1980, 1, 39–69.

Tversky, A., and Kahneman, D., The Framing of Decisions and the Psychology of Choice, Science, 1981, 211, 453–458.

Vinoker, A. Review and theoretical analysis of the effects of group processes upon individual and group decisions involving risk. Psychological Bulletin, 1971, 76, 234–250.

von Neumann, J. and Morgenstern, O. Theory of games and economic behavior, Princeton: Princeton University Press, 1947.